FORWARD/COMMENTARY

The National Institute of Standards and Technology (NIST) is a measurement standards laboratory, and a non-regulatory agency of the **United States Department of Commerce**. Its mission is to promote innovation and industrial competitiveness. Founded in 1901, as the National Bureau of Standards, NIST was formed with the mandate to provide standard weights and measures, and to serve as the national physical laboratory for the United States. With a world-class measurement and testing laboratory encompassing a wide range of areas of computer science, mathematics, statistics, and systems engineering, NIST's cybersecurity program supports its overall mission to promote U.S. innovation and industrial competitiveness by advancing measurement science, standards, and related technology through research and development in ways that enhance economic security and improve our quality of life.

The need for cybersecurity standards and best practices that address interoperability, usability and privacy has been shown to be critical for the nation. NIST's cybersecurity programs seek to enable greater development and application of practical, innovative security technologies and methodologies that enhance the country's ability to address current and future computer and information security challenges.

The cybersecurity publications produced by NIST cover a wide range of cybersecurity concepts that are carefully designed to work together to produce a holistic approach to cybersecurity primarily for government agencies and constitute the best practices used by industry. This holistic strategy to cybersecurity covers the gamut of security subjects from development of secure encryption standards for communication and storage of information while at rest to how best to recover from a cyber-attack.

The field of computer science is rapidly changing from the basic personal computer to the "Internet of Things". Many of these devices were not designed to be "connected" and very little thought was given to secure them from cyber-attack. Recent events have clearly demonstrated the need to secure everything from web cams to electrical utility grids.

That's where NIST comes in. Just as the National Bureau of Standards set the standard for weights and measures at the beginning of the last century, the 21st century mission for NIST is to set the standard for cybersecurity. NIST gathers the very best minds in industry and government and serves as the central clearing house for information that sets the standard for security for the nation. This publication is only one piece in the mosaic of publications NIST produces but each is a vital key in its own field to the overall cybersecurity strategy that government and industry must adopt in the public interest. All NIST publications are freely available for download over the internet to maximize adoption of the standards.

This NIST Special Publication is an integral part of the overall design, development and maintenance of an IT security infrastructure that ensures confidentiality, integrity, and availability of mission critical information. It was developed to assist in choosing IT security products that meet an organization's requirements. It should be used with other NIST publications to develop a comprehensive approach to managing, satisfying, and verifying an organization's IT security and information assurance requirements.

We here at 4th Watch Books are former government employees so we know how government employees actually use the standards. When a new standard is released, an engineer prints it out, punches holes and puts it in a 3-ring binder. While this is not a big deal for a 5 or 10-page document, many NIST documents are over 100 pages and printing a large document is a time-consuming effort. Unfortunately, reductions in government over the years means that now the engineer himself has to print his own copy (no one has a secretary anymore). So, an engineer that's paid $75 an hour is spending hours simply printing out the tools he needs to do his job. That's time that could be better spent doing engineering.

4th Watch Books prints these documents so engineers can focus on what they were hired to do – engineering. This is important because there are not as many engineers working in government as there used to be, so wasted time on clerical duties is unproductive. As a former senior leader in the government, I always encouraged my subordinates to look for ways to do things better, faster, cheaper. I always asked my staff to focus on the objective and consider the cost/benefit analysis of everything they do. If something can be done better, faster and cheaper, then we would be remiss if we didn't take advantage of the opportunity.

This book is a perfect example of that type of thinking. Rather than spend the limited resources we have at a particular agency to develop cybersecurity solutions, it will always be better, faster and cheaper to embrace a standard that has been fully-developed and totally integrated in the wider scheme of things by the engineers at NIST with the help they receive from industry.

Luis Ayala
Writer and Publisher, 4th Watch Books

Mr. Ayala began his career in 1970 when he was drafted during the Vietnam Police Action and served 4 years in the U.S. Air Force, Strategic Air Command. With 40+ years of experience, he has led multi-million dollar federal programs for USACE, NAVFAC, GSA, and the Intelligence Community. He is a former Senior Technical Expert at the Defense Intelligence Agency with in-depth technical experience. He is an avid writer on the subject of the threats of cyber-physical attacks on America.

NIST Special Publication 800-60 Volume I
Revision 1

**National Institute of
Standards and Technology**
U.S. Department of Commerce

Volume I:
Guide for Mapping Types of Information and Information Systems to Security Categories

Kevin Stine
Rich Kissel
William C. Barker
Jim Fahlsing
Jessica Gulick

INFORMATION SECURITY

Computer Security Division
Information Technology Laboratory
National Institute of Standards and Technology
Gaithersburg, MD 20899-8930

August 2008

U.S. DEPARTMENT OF COMMERCE
Carlos M. Gutierrez, Secretary

NATIONAL INSTITUTE OF STANDARDS AND TECHNOLOGY
James M. Turner, Deputy Director

Reports on Computer Systems Technology

The Information Technology Laboratory (ITL) at the National Institute of Standards and Technology (NIST) promotes the U.S. economy and public welfare by providing technical leadership for the nation's measurement and standards infrastructure. ITL develops tests, test methods, reference data, proof-of-concept implementations, and technical analyses to advance the development and productive use of information technology. ITL's responsibilities include the development of management, administrative, technical, and physical standards and guidelines for the cost-effective security and privacy of other than national security-related information in federal information systems. This Special Publication 800-series reports on ITL's research, guidelines, and outreach efforts in information system security and its collaborative activities with industry, government, and academic organizations.

Authority

This document has been developed by the National Institute of Standards and Technology (NIST) to further its statutory responsibilities under the Federal Information Security Management Act (FISMA) of 2002, P.L. 107-347. NIST is responsible for developing standards and guidelines, including minimum requirements, for providing adequate information security for all agency operations and assets but such standards and guidelines shall not apply to national security systems. This guideline is consistent with the requirements of the Office of Management and Budget (OMB) Circular A-130, Section 8b(3), *Securing Agency Information Systems*, as analyzed in A-130, Appendix IV: *Analysis of Key Sections*. Supplemental information is provided in A-130, Appendix III.

This guideline has been prepared for use by federal agencies. It may also be used by nongovernmental organizations on a voluntary basis and is not subject to copyright. (Attribution would be appreciated by NIST.)

Nothing in this document should be taken to contradict standards and guidelines made mandatory and binding on federal agencies by the Secretary of Commerce under statutory authority. Nor should these guidelines be interpreted as altering or superseding the existing authorities of the Secretary of Commerce, Director of the OMB, or any other federal official.

NIST Special Publication 800-60 Volume I, Revision 1, 53 pages

(Date) CODEN: NSPUE2

COMMENTS MAY BE SUBMITTED TO THE COMPUTER SECURITY DIVISION, INFORMATION TECHNOLOGY LABORATORY, NIST VIA ELECTRONIC MAIL AT SEC-CERT@NIST.GOV OR VIA REGULAR MAIL AT 100 BUREAU DRIVE (MAIL STOP 8930), GAITHERSBURG, MD 20899-8930

Acknowledgements

The authors, Kevin Stine, Rich Kissel, and William C. Barker, wish to thank their colleagues, Jim Fahlsing and Jessica Gulick from Science Applications International Corporation (SAIC), who helped update this document, prepare drafts, and review materials. In addition, special thanks are due to our reviewers, Arnold Johnson (NIST), Karen Quigg (Mitre Corporation), and Ruth Bandler (Food and Drug Administration), who greatly contributed to the document's development. A special note of thanks goes to Elizabeth Lennon for her superb technical editing and administrative support. NIST also gratefully acknowledges and appreciates the many contributions from individuals in the public and private sectors whose thoughtful and constructive comments improved the quality and usefulness of this publication.

Volume I: Guide for Mapping Types of Information and Information Systems to Security Categories

Table of Contents

EXECUTIVE SUMMARY

Title III of the E-Government Act (Public Law 107-347), titled the Federal Information Security Management Act (FISMA), tasked the National Institute of Standards and Technology (NIST) to develop:

- Standards to be used by all Federal agencies to categorize all information and information systems collected or maintained by or on behalf of each agency based on the objectives of providing appropriate levels of information security according to a range of risk levels;

- Guidelines recommending the types of information and information systems to be included in each such category; and

- Minimum information security requirements (i.e., management, operational, and technical security controls), for information and information systems in each such category.

In response to the second of these tasks, this guideline has been developed to assist Federal government agencies to categorize information and information systems. The guideline's objective is to facilitate application of appropriate levels of information security according to a range of levels of impact or consequences that might result from the unauthorized disclosure, modification, or use of the information or information system. This guideline assumes that the user is familiar with *Standards for Security Categorization of Federal Information and Information Systems* (Federal Information Processing Standard [FIPS] 199). The guideline and its appendices:

- Review the security categorization terms and definitions established by FIPS 199;

- Recommend a security categorization process;

- Describe a methodology for identifying types of Federal information and information systems;

- Suggest provisional[1] security impact levels for common information types;

- Discuss information attributes that may result in variances from the provisional impact level assignment; and

- Describe how to establish a system security categorization based on the system's use, connectivity, and aggregate information content.

This document is intended as a reference resource rather than as a tutorial and not all of the material will be relevant to all agencies. This document includes two volumes, a basic guideline and a volume of appendices. Users should review the guidelines provided in Volume I, then refer to only that specific material from the appendices that applies to their own systems and applications. The provisional impact assignments are provided in Volume II, Appendix C and D. The basis employed in this guideline for the identification of information types is the Office of

---

[1] Provisional security impact levels are the initial or conditional impact determinations made until all considerations are fully reviewed, analyzed, and accepted in the subsequent categorization steps by appropriate officials.

Management and Budget's Federal Enterprise Architecture (FEA) Program Management Office (PMO) October 2007 publication, *The Consolidated Reference Model Document Version 2.3.*

1.0 INTRODUCTION

The identification of information processed on an information system is essential to the proper selection of security controls and ensuring the confidentiality, integrity, and availability of the system and its information. The National Institute of Standards and Technology (NIST) Special Publication (SP) 800-60 has been developed to assist Federal government agencies to categorize information and information systems.

1.1 Purpose and Applicability

NIST SP 800-60 addresses the FISMA direction to develop guidelines recommending the types of information and information systems to be included in each category of potential security impact. This guideline is intended to help agencies consistently map security impact levels to types of: (i) information (e.g., privacy, medical, proprietary, financial, contractor sensitive, trade secret, investigation); and (ii) information systems (e.g., mission critical, mission support, administrative). This guideline applies to all Federal information systems other than *national security systems*. *National security systems* store, process, or communicate *national security* information.[2]

1.2 Target Audience

This publication is intended to serve a diverse federal audience of information system and information security professionals including: (i) individuals with information system and information security management and oversight responsibilities (e.g., chief information officers, senior agency information security officers, authorizing officials); (ii) organizational officials having a vested interest in the accomplishment of organizational missions (e.g., mission and business area owners, information owners); (iii) individuals with information system development responsibilities (e.g., program and project managers, information system developers); and (iv) individuals with information security implementation and operational responsibilities (e.g., information system owners, information owners, information system security officers).

1.3 Relationship to Other Documents

NIST Special Publication (SP) 800-60 is a member of the NIST family of security-related publications including:

- FIPS Publication 199, *Standards for Security Categorization of Federal Information and Information Systems;*

- FIPS Publication 200, *Minimum Security Requirements for Federal Information and Information Systems;*

---

[2] FISMA defines a *national security system* as any information system (including telecommunications system) used or operated by an agency or by a contractor on behalf of an agency, or any other organization on behalf of an agency – (i) the function, operation, or use of which: involves intelligence activities; involves cryptologic activities related to national security; involves command and control of military forces; involves equipment that is an integral part of a weapon or weapon system; or is critical to the direct fulfillment of military or intelligence missions (excluding a routine administrative or business system used for applications such as payroll, finance, logistics, and personnel management); or (ii) that processes classified information. [See Public Law 107-347, Section 3542 (b)(2)(A).]

- NIST SP 800-30, *Risk Management Guide for Information Technology Systems;*[3]

- NIST SP 800-37, *Guide for the Security Certification and Accreditation of Federal Information Systems;*

- NIST Draft SP 800-39, *Managing Risk from Information Systems: An Organization Perspective;*

- NIST SP 800-53, *Recommended Security Controls for Federal Information Systems;*

- NIST SP 800-53A, *Guide for Assessing the Security Controls in Federal Information Systems*; and

- NIST SP 800-59, *Guideline for Identifying an Information System as a National Security System.*

This series of nine documents is intended to provide a structured, yet flexible framework for selecting, specifying, employing, evaluating, and monitoring the security controls in Federal information systems—and thus, makes a significant contribution toward satisfying the requirements of the Federal Information Security Management Act (FISMA) of 2002. While the publications are mutually reinforcing and have some dependencies, in most cases, they can be effectively used independently of one another.

The SP 800-60 information types and associated security impact levels are based on the Office of Management and Budget (OMB) Federal Enterprise Architecture Program Management Office's October 2007 *FEA Consolidated Reference Model Document, Version 2.3,* inputs from participants in previous NIST SP 800-60 workshops, and FIPS 199. Rationale for the example impact-level recommendations provided in the appendices has been derived from multiple sources and, as such, will require several iterations of review, comment, and subsequent modification to achieve consistency in terminology, structure, and content.

1.4 Organization of this Special Publication

This is Volume I of two volumes. It contains the basic guidelines for mapping types of information and information systems to security categories. The appendices, including security categorization recommendations for mission-based information types and rationale for security categorization recommendations, are published as a separate Volume II.

Volume I provides the following background information and mapping guidelines:

- Section 2: Provides an overview of the value of the categorization process to agency missions, security programs and overall information technology (IT) management and the publication's role in the system development lifecycle, the certification and accreditation process, and the NIST Risk Management Framework.

- Section 3: Provides the security objectives and corresponding security impact levels identified in the Federal Information Processing Standard 199, *Standards for Security Categorization of Federal Information and Information Systems* [FIPS 199];

---

[3] This document is currently under revision and will be reissued as Special Publication 800-30, Revision 1, *Guide for Conducting Risk Assessments.*

- Section 4: Identifies the process including guidelines for identification of *mission-based* and *management and support* information types and the process used to select security impact levels, general considerations relating to security impact assignment, guidelines for system security categorization, and considerations and guidelines for applying and interrelating system categorization results to the agency's enterprise, large supporting infrastructures, and interconnecting systems;

- Appendix A: Glossary; and

- Appendix B: References.

Volume II includes the following appendices:

- Appendix A: Glossary [Repeated];

- Appendix B: References [Repeated];

- Appendix C: Provisional security impact level assignments and supporting rationale for *management and support* information (administrative, management, and service information);

- Appendix D: Provisional security impact level assignments and supporting rationale for *mission-based* information (mission information and services delivery mechanisms); and

- Appendix E: Legislative and executive sources that specify sensitivity/criticality properties.

2.0 PUBLICATION OVERVIEW

Security categorization provides a vital step in integrating security into the government agency's business and information technology management functions and establishes the foundation for security standardization amongst their information systems. Security categorization starts with the identification of what information supports which government lines of business, as defined by the Federal Enterprise Architecture (FEA). Subsequent steps focus on the evaluation of the need for security in terms of confidentiality, integrity, and availability. The result is strong linkage between missions, information, and information systems with cost effective information security.

2.1 Agencies Support the Security Categorization Process

Agencies support the categorization process by establishing mission-based information types for the organization. The approach to establishing mission-based information types at an agency begins by documenting the agency's mission and business areas. In the case of mission-based information, the responsible individuals, in coordination with management, operational, enterprise architecture, and security stakeholders, should compile a comprehensive set of the agency's lines of business and mission areas. In addition, responsible individuals should identify the applicable sub-functions necessary to accomplish the organization's mission. For example, one organization's mission might be related to economic development. Sub-functions that are part of the organization's economic development mission might include business and industry development, intellectual property protection, or financial sector oversight. Each of these sub-functions represents an information type.

Agencies should conduct FIPS 199 security categorizations of their information systems as an agency-wide activity with the involvement of the senior leadership and other key officials within the organization (e.g., mission and business owners, authorizing officials, risk executive, chief information officer, senior agency information security officer, information system owners, and information owners) to ensure that each information system receives the appropriate management oversight and reflects the needs of the organization as a whole. Senior leadership oversight in the security categorization process is essential so that the next steps in the NIST Risk Management Framework[4] (e.g., security control selection) can be carried out in an effective and consistent manner throughout the agency.

2.2 Value to Agency Missions, Security Programs and IT Management

Federal agencies are heavily dependent upon information and information systems to successfully conduct critical missions. With an increasing reliability on and growing complexity of information systems as well as a constantly changing risk environment, information security has become a mission-essential function. This function must be conducted in a manner that reduces the risks to the information entrusted to the agency, its overall mission, and its ability to do business and to serve the American public. In the end, information security, as a function, becomes a business enabler through diligent and effective management of risk to information confidentiality, integrity, and availability.

---

[4] See Section 2.5, Figure 1: NIST Risk Management Framework

Therefore, the value of information security categorization is to enable agencies to proactively implement appropriate information security controls based on the assessed potential impact to information confidentiality, integrity, and availability and in turn to support their mission in a cost-effective manner. An incorrect information system impact analysis (i.e., incorrect FIPS 199 security categorization) can result in the agency either over protecting the information system thus wasting valuable security resources, or under protecting the information system and placing important operations and assets at risk. The aggregation of such mistakes at the enterprise level can further compound the problem.

In contrast, conducting FIPS 199 impact analyses as an agency-wide exercise with the participation of key officials (e.g., Chief Information Officer [CIO], Senior Agency Information Security Officer [SAISO], Authorizing Officials, Mission/System Owners) at multiple levels can enable the agency to leverage economies of scale through the effective management and implementation of security controls at the enterprise level. A resulting value of consistently implementing this systematic process for determining the security categorization and the application of appropriate security protection is an improved overall understanding of the agency's mission, business processes, and information and system ownership.

Implementation Tip

To enable an appropriate level of mission support and the diligent implementation of current and future information security requirements, each agency should establish a formal process to validate system level security categorizations in terms of agency priorities. This will not only promote comparable evaluation of systems, but also yield added benefits to include leveraging common security controls and establishing defense-in-depth.

2.3 Role in the System Development Lifecycle

An initial security categorization should occur early in the agency's system development lifecycle (SDLC). The resulting security categorization would feed into security requirements identification (later to evolve into security controls) and other related activities such as privacy impact analysis or critical infrastructure analysis. Ultimately, the identified security requirements and selected security controls are introduced to the standard systems engineering process to effectively integrate the security controls with the information systems functional and operational requirements, as well as other pertinent system requirements (e.g., reliability, maintainability, supportability).

2.4 Role in the Certification and Accreditation Process

Security categorization establishes the foundation of the certification and accreditation (C&A) activity by determining the levels of rigor required for certification and overall assurance testing of security controls, as well as additional activities that may be needed (i.e., privacy and critical infrastructure protection (CIP)). Thus, it assists in determining C&A level of effort and associated activity duration.

Security categorization is a prerequisite activity for the C&A process. The categorization should be revisited at least every three years or when significant change occurs to the system or supporting business lines. Situational changes outside the system or agency may require a reevaluation of the categorization (i.e., directed mission changes, changes in governance, elevated or targeted threat activities). For more information, see NIST SP 800-64, *Security Considerations in the Information System Development Life Cycle* and NIST SP 800-37, *Guide for the Security Certification and Accreditation of Federal Information Systems*.

Implementation Tip

It is important to routinely revisit the security categorization as the mission/ business changes because it is likely the impact levels or even information types may change as well.

2.5 Role in the NIST Risk Management Framework

Security Categorization is the key first step in the Risk Management Framework[5] because of its effect on all other steps in the framework from selection of security controls to level of effort in assessing security control effectiveness.

Figure 1, NIST Risk Management Framework, depicts the role of NIST security standards and guidelines for information system security.

---

[5] NIST SP 800-39, *Managing Risk from Information Systems: An Organizational Perspective,* (Initial Public Draft), October 2007.

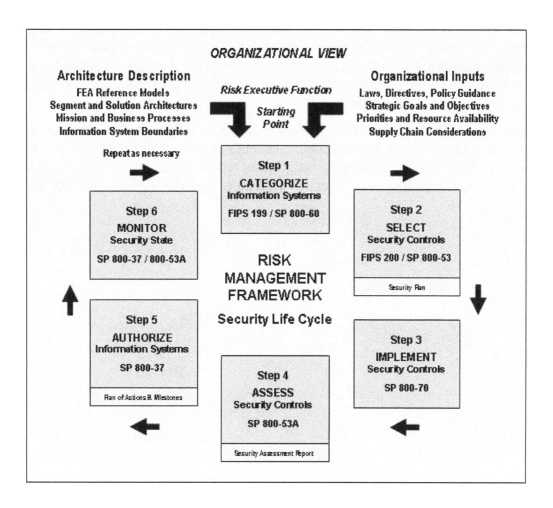

Figure 1: NIST Risk Management Framework

The security categorization process documented in this publication provides input into the following processes:

- Step 2: Select an initial set of security controls for the information system based on the FIPS 199 security categorization and apply tailoring guidance as appropriate, to obtain a starting point for required controls as specified in FIPS 200, *Minimum Security Requirements for Federal Information and Information Systems* and NIST SP 800-53, *Recommended Security Controls for Federal Information Systems.* Utilizing NIST SP 800-53 and SP 800-30, *Risk Management Guide for Information Technology Systems,* supplement the initial set of tailored security controls based on an assessment of risk and local conditions including organization-specific security requirements, specific threat information, cost-benefit analyses, or special circumstances.

- Step 3: Implement the security controls in the information system.

- Step 4: Assess the security controls using appropriate methods and procedures to determine the extent to which the controls are implemented correctly, operating as intended, and producing the desired outcome with respect to meeting the security requirements for the system. (Reference NIST SP 800-53A, *Guide for Assessing the Security Controls in Federal Information Systems*).

- Step 5: Authorize information system operation based upon a determination of the risk to organizational operations, organizational assets, or to individuals resulting from the operation of the information system and the decision that this risk is acceptable as specified in NIST SP 800-37, *Guide for the Security Certification and Accreditation of Federal Information Systems.*

- Step 6: Monitor and assess selected security controls in the information system on a continuous basis including documenting changes to the system, conducting security impact analyses of the associated changes, and reporting the security status of the system to appropriate organizational officials on a regular basis. (Reference NIST SP 800-37 and SP 800-53A).

3.0 SECURITY CATEGORIZATION OF INFORMATION AND INFORMATION SYSTEMS

Federal Information Processing Standard 199 (FIPS 199), *Standards for Security Categorization of Federal Information and Information Systems*, defines the security categories, security objectives, and impact levels to which SP 800-60 maps information types. FIPS 199 establishes security categories based on the magnitude of harm expected to result from compromises rather than on the results of an assessment that includes an attempt to determine the probability of compromise. FIPS 199 also describes the context of use for this guideline. Some of the content of FIPS 199 is included in this section in order to simplify the use of this guideline.

3.1 Security Categories and Objectives

3.1.1 Security Categories

FIPS 199 establishes security categories for both information[6] and information systems. The security categories are based on the potential impact on an organization should certain events occur. The potential impacts could jeopardize the information and information systems needed by the organization to accomplish its assigned mission, protect its assets, fulfill its legal responsibilities, maintain its day-to-day functions, and protect individuals. Security categories are to be used in conjunction with vulnerability and threat information in assessing the risk to an organization.

FIPS 199 establishes three potential levels of impact (low, moderate, and high) relevant to securing Federal information and information systems for each of three stated security objectives (confidentiality, integrity, and availability).

3.1.2 Security Objectives and Types of Potential Losses

As reflected in Table 1, FISMA and FIPS 199 define three security objectives for information and information systems.

Table 1: Information and Information System Security Objectives

Security Objectives	FISMA Definition [44 U.S.C., Sec. 3542]	FIPS 199 Definition
Confidentiality	"Preserving authorized restrictions on information access and disclosure, including means for protecting personal privacy and proprietary information…"	A loss of *confidentiality* is the unauthorized disclosure of information.
Integrity	"Guarding against improper information modification or destruction, and includes ensuring information non-repudiation and authenticity…"	A loss of *integrity* is the unauthorized modification or destruction of information.
Availability	"Ensuring timely and reliable access to and use of information…"	A loss of *availability* is the disruption of access to or use of information or an information system.

---

[6] Information is categorized according to its *information type*. An information type is a specific category of information (e.g., privacy, medical, proprietary, financial, investigative, contractor sensitive, security management) defined by an organization or, in some instances, by a specific law, Executive Order, directive, policy, or regulation.

3.2 Impact Assessment

FIPS 199 defines three levels of *potential impact* on organizations or individuals should there be a breach of security (i.e., a loss of confidentiality, integrity, or availability). The application of these definitions must take place within the context of each organization and the overall national interest. Table 2 provides FIPS 199 potential impact definitions.

Table 2: Potential Impact Levels

Potential Impact	Definitions
Low	The potential impact is **low** if—The loss of confidentiality, integrity, or availability could be expected to have a **limited** adverse effect on organizational operations, organizational assets, or individuals.[7]
	A limited adverse effect means that, for example, the loss of confidentiality, integrity, or availability might: (i) cause a degradation in mission capability to an extent and duration that the organization is able to perform its primary functions, but the effectiveness of the functions is noticeably reduced; (ii) result in minor damage to organizational assets; (iii) result in minor financial loss; or (iv) result in minor harm to individuals.
Moderate	The potential impact is **moderate** if—The loss of confidentiality, integrity, or availability could be expected to have a **serious** adverse effect on organizational operations, organizational assets, or individuals.
	A serious adverse effect means that, for example, the loss of confidentiality, integrity, or availability might: (i) cause a significant degradation in mission capability to an extent and duration that the organization is able to perform its primary functions, but the effectiveness of the functions is significantly reduced; (ii) result in significant damage to organizational assets; (iii) result in significant financial loss; or (iv) result in significant harm to individuals that does not involve loss of life or serious life threatening injuries.
High	The potential impact is **high** if—The loss of confidentiality, integrity, or availability could be expected to have a **severe or catastrophic** adverse effect on organizational operations, organizational assets, or individuals.
	A severe or catastrophic adverse effect means that, for example, the loss of confidentiality, integrity, or availability might: (i) cause a severe degradation in or loss of mission capability to an extent and duration that the organization is not able to perform one or more of its primary functions; (ii) result in major damage to organizational assets; (iii) result in major financial loss; or (iv) result in severe or catastrophic harm to individuals involving loss of life or serious life threatening injuries.

In FIPS 199, the security category of an information type can be associated with both user information and system information[8] and can be applicable to information in either electronic or non-electronic form. It is also used as input in considering the appropriate security category for a system. Establishing an appropriate security category for an information type simply requires determining the *potential impact* for each security objective associated with the particular information type. The generalized format for expressing the security category, or *SC*, of an information type is:

---

[7] Adverse effects on individuals may include, but are not limited to, loss of the privacy to which individuals are entitled under law.

[8] System information (e.g., network routing tables, password files, cryptographic key management information) must be protected at a level commensurate with the most critical or sensitive user information being processed by the information system to ensure confidentiality, integrity, and availability.

Security Category $_{\text{information type}}$ = {(confidentiality, impact), (integrity, impact), (availability, impact)}

where the acceptable values for potential *impact* are low, moderate, high, or not applicable.[9]

---

[9] The potential impact value of *not applicable* may be applied only to the confidentiality security objective.

4.0 ASSIGNMENT OF IMPACT LEVELS AND SECURITY CATEGORIZATION

This section provides a methodology for assigning security impact levels and security categorizations for information types and information systems consistent with the organization's assigned mission and business functions based on FIPS 199, Standards for Security Categorization of Federal Information and Information Systems. This document assumes that the user has read and is familiar with FIPS 199. Figure 2 illustrates the four-step security categorization process and how it drives the selection of baseline security controls.

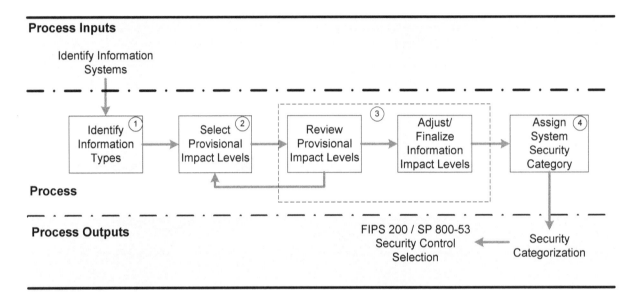

Figure 2: SP 800-60 Security Categorization Process Execution

Table 3 provides a step-by-step roadmap for identifying information types, establishing security impact levels for loss of confidentiality, integrity, and availability of information types, and assigning security categorization for the information types and for the information systems. Security categorization is the basis for identifying an initial baseline set of security controls for the information system.[10] Each functional step in the process is explained in detail in Sections 4.1 through 4.4.

---

[10] An information system is a discrete set of information resources organized for the collection, processing, maintenance, use, sharing, dissemination, or disposition of information [Source: SP 800-53; FIPS 200; FIPS 199; 44 U.S.C., Sec. 3502; OMB Circular A-130, App. III]

Table 3: SP 800-60 Process Roadmap

Process Step	Activities	Roles
Input: Identify information systems	• Agencies should develop their own policies regarding information system identification for security categorization purposes. The system is generally bounded by a security perimeter[11].	CIO; SAISO; Mission Owners

Step 1
 Identify Information Types
	• Document the agency's business and mission areas
	 • Identify all of the information types that are input, stored, processed, and/or output from each system [Section 4.1]
	    o Identify *Mission–based* Information Type categories based on supporting FEA Lines of Business [Section 4.1.1]
	    o As applicable, identify *Management and Support* Information Type categories based on supporting FEA Lines of Business [Section 4.1.2]
	    o Specify applicable sub-functions for the identified *Mission-based* and *Management and Support* categories [Volume II, Appendices C and D]
	    o As necessary, identify other required information types [Sections 4.1.3, 4.1.4]
	 • Document applicable information types for the identified information system along with the basis for the information type selection [Section 4.5]
		Mission Owners; Information Owners

Step 2
 Select Provisional Impact Levels
	• Select the security impact levels for the identified information types
	    o from the recommended provisional impact levels for each identified information type [Volume II, Appendices C and D)
	    o or, from FIPS 199 criteria provided in Table 7 Section 4.2.1, and Section 4.2.2
	 • Determine the security category (SC) for each information type: SC $_{\text{information type}}$ = {(confidentiality, impact), (integrity, impact), (availability, impact)}
	 • Document the provisional impact level of confidentiality, integrity, and availability associated with the system's information type [Section 4.5]
		Information System Security Officer (ISSO)

Step 3
 Review Provisional Impact Levels
 	
 Adjust/ Finalize Information Impact Levels
	• Review the appropriateness of the provisional impact levels based on the organization, environment, mission, use, and data sharing [Section 4.3]
	 • Adjust the impact levels as necessary based on the following considerations:
	    o Confidentiality, integrity, and availability factors [Section 4.2.2]
	    o Situational and operational drivers (timing, lifecycle, etc.) [Section 4.3]
	    o Legal or statutory reasons
	 • Document all adjustments to the impact levels and provide the rationale or justification for the adjustments [Section 4.5]
		SAISO; ISSO; Mission Owners; Information Owners

Step 4 Assign System Security Category	• Review identified security categorizations for the aggregate of information types. • Determine the system security categorization by identifying the security impact level high water mark for each of the security objectives (confidentiality, integrity, availability): SC $_{\text{System X}}$ = {(confidentiality, impact), (integrity, impact), (availability, impact)} • Adjust the security impact level high water mark for each system security objective, as necessary, by applying the factors discussed in section 4.4.2. • Assign the overall information system impact level based on the highest impact level for the system security objectives (confidentiality, integrity, availability) • Follow the agency's oversight process for reviewing, approving, and documenting all determinations or decisions [Section 4.5]	CIO, SAISO; ISSO; Mission Owners; Information Owners
Output: Security Categorization	• Output that can be used as input to the selection of the set of security controls necessary for each system and the system risk assessment • The minimum security controls recommended for each system security category can be found in NIST SP 800-53, as updated	CIO; ISSO; Authorizing Officials; Developers

---

[11] Security perimeter is synonymous with the term accreditation boundary and includes all components of an information system to be accredited by an authorizing official and excludes separately accredited systems to which the information system is connected.

13

4.1 Step 1: Identify Information Types

In accordance with FIPS 199, agencies shall identify all of the applicable information types that are representative of input, stored, processed, and/or output data from each system. The initial activity in mapping types of Federal information and information systems to security objectives and impact levels is the development of an information taxonomy, or creation of a catalog of information types.[12] The basis for the identification of information types is the OMB's Business Reference Model (BRM) described in the October 2007 publication, *FEA Consolidated Reference Model Document, Version 2.3*. The *BRM* describes four business areas containing 39 FEA lines of business.[13] The four business areas separate government operations into high-level categories relating:

- The purpose of government (*services for citizens*);
- The mechanisms the government uses to achieve its purpose (*mode of delivery*);
- The support functions necessary to conduct government operations (*support delivery of services*); and
- The resource management functions that support all areas of the government's business (*management of government resources*).

The first two business areas, *services for citizens* and the *mode of delivery* represent the NIST SP 800-60 Mission-based Information Types and will be discussed first in the following section, while *support delivery of services* and *management of government resources* represent Management and Support Information Types and will be presented in Section 4.1.2.

Although this guideline identifies a number of information types and bases its taxonomy on the *BRM*, only a few of the types identified are likely to be processed by any single system. Also, each system may process information that does not fall neatly into one of the listed information types. Once a set of information types identified in this guideline has been selected, it is prudent to review the information processed by each system under review to see if additional types need to be identified for impact assessment purposes. Also, it is recommended that organizational officials maintain proper documentation of identified information types per information system along with the basis for the information type selection. Guidance for documenting information types is provided in Section 4.5.

4.1.1 Identification of Mission-based Information Types

This section describes a process for identifying mission-based information types and for specifying the impact of unauthorized disclosure, modification, or unavailability of this information. Mission-based information types are, by definition, specific to individual departments and agencies or to specific sets of departments and agencies. The BRM *services for citizens* business area provides the primary frame of reference for determining the security

---

[12] One issue associated with the taxonomy activity is the determination of the degree of granularity. If the categories are too broad, then the guidelines for assigning impact levels are likely to be too general to be useful. On the other hand, if an attempt is made to provide guidelines for each element of information processed by each government agency, the guideline is likely to be unwieldy and to require excessively frequent changes.

[13] Definitions are provided in SP 800-60 Appendix A for the BRM terms such as "Business Areas", "Lines of Businesses" and "Sub-functions".

objectives impact levels for mission-based information and information systems. The consequences or impact of unauthorized disclosure of information, modification or destruction of information, and disruption of access to or use of information are defined by the nature and beneficiary of the service being provided or supported. The BRM establishes 26 direct services and delivery support lines of business with 98 associated information types (reference Table 4). Two additional information types were included to address Executive Functions of the Executive Office of the President and Trade Law Enforcement. These additions are identified by italics in Table 4.

Table 4: Mission-Based Information Types and Delivery Mechanisms[14]

Mission Areas and Information Types [Services for Citizens]		
D.1 Defense & National Security	**D.7 Energy**	**D.14 Health**
Strategic National & Theater Defense	Energy Supply	Access to Care
Operational Defense	Energy Conservation and Preparedness	Population Health Mgmt & Consumer
Tactical Defense	Energy Resource Management	Safety
D.2 Homeland Security	Energy Production	Health Care Administration
Border and Transportation Security	**D.8 Environmental Management**	Health Care Delivery Services
Key Asset and Critical Infrastructure	Environmental Monitoring and	Health Care Research and Practitioner
Protection	Forecasting	Education
Catastrophic Defense	Environmental Remediation	**D.15 Income Security**
Executive Functions of the Executive	Pollution Prevention and Control	General Retirement and Disability
Office of the President (EOP)	**D.9 Economic Development**	Unemployment Compensation
D.3 Intelligence Operations	Business and Industry Development	Housing Assistance
Intelligence Planning	Intellectual Property Protection	Food and Nutrition Assistance
Intelligence Collection	Financial Sector Oversight	Survivor Compensation
Intelligence Analysis & Production	Industry Sector Income Stabilization	**D.16 Law Enforcement**
Intelligence Dissemination	**D.10 Community & Social Services**	Criminal Apprehension
Intelligence Processing	Homeownership Promotion	Criminal Investigation and Surveillance
D.4 Disaster Management	Community and Regional Development	Citizen Protection
Disaster Monitoring and Prediction	Social Services	Leadership Protection
Disaster Preparedness and Planning	Postal Services	Property Protection
Disaster Repair and Restoration	**D.11 Transportation**	Substance Control
Emergency Response	Ground Transportation	Crime Prevention
D.5 International Affairs &	Water Transportation	*Trade Law Enforcement*
Commerce	Air Transportation	**D.17 Litigation & Judicial Activities**
Foreign Affairs	Space Operations	Judicial Hearings
International Development and	**D.12 Education**	Legal Defense
Humanitarian Aid	Elementary, Secondary, and Vocational	Legal Investigation
Global Trade	Education	Legal Prosecution and Litigation
D.6 Natural Resources	Higher Education	Resolution Facilitation
Water Resource Management	Cultural and Historic Preservation	**D.18 Federal Correctional Activities**
Conservation, Marine and Land	Cultural and Historic Exhibition	Criminal Incarceration
Management	**D.13 Workforce Management**	Criminal Rehabilitation
Recreational Resource Management and	Training and Employment	**D.19 General Sciences & Innovation**
Tourism	Labor Rights Management	Scientific and Technological Research
Agricultural Innovation and Services	Worker Safety	and Innovation
		Space Exploration and Innovation

---

[14] The recommended information types provided in NIST SP 800-60 are established from the "business areas" and "lines of business" from OMB's Business Reference Model (BRM) section of Federal Enterprise Architecture (FEA) Consolidated Reference Model Document Version 2.3, October 2007.

Table 4: Mission-Based Information Types and Delivery Mechanisms[14]

Services Delivery Mechanisms and Information Types [Mode of Delivery]		
D.20 Knowledge Creation & Management	**D.22 Public Goods Creation & Management**	**D.24 Credit and Insurance**
Research and Development	Manufacturing	Direct Loans
General Purpose Data and Statistics	Construction	Loan Guarantees
Advising and Consulting	Public Resources, Facility and	General Insurance
Knowledge Dissemination	Infrastructure Management	**D.25 Transfers to State/ Local**
D.21 Regulatory Compliance & Enforcement	Information Infrastructure Management	**Governments**
	D.23 Federal Financial Assistance	Formula Grants
Inspections and Auditing	Federal Grants (Non-State)	Project/Competitive Grants
Standards Setting/Reporting Guideline	Direct Transfers to Individuals	Earmarked Grants
Development	Subsidies	State Loans
Permits and Licensing	Tax Credits	**D.26 Direct Services for Citizens**
		Military Operations
		Civilian Operations

The approach to establishing mission-based information types at an agency level begins by documenting the agency's business and mission areas. The owner, or designee, of each information system is responsible for identifying the information types stored in, processed by, or generated by that information system. In the case of mission-based information, the responsible individuals, in coordination with management, operational, and security stakeholders, should compile a comprehensive set of lines of business and mission areas conducted by the agency. In addition, the responsible individuals should identify the applicable sub-functions necessary to conduct agency business and in turn accomplish the agency's mission. For example, one mission conducted by an agency might be law enforcement. Sub-functions that are part of the agency's law enforcement mission might include criminal investigation and surveillance, criminal apprehension, criminal incarceration, citizen protection, crime prevention, and property protection. Each of these sub-functions would represent an information type.

Recommended mission-based lines of business and constituent sub-functions that may be processed by information systems are identified in Table 4 with details provided in Volume II, Appendix D, "Examples of Impact Determination for Mission-based Information and Information Systems."

Implementation Tip

At the agency level, all government agencies perform at least one of the *mission areas* and employ at least one of the *services delivery mechanisms* described in Table 4. However, some information systems may only provide a supporting role to the agency's mission and not directly process any of the *mission-based* information types.

4.1.2   Identification of Management and Support Information

Much Federal government information and many supporting information systems are not employed directly to provide direct mission-based services, but are primarily intended to support delivery of services or to manage resources. The *support delivery of services* and *management of resources* business areas are together composed of 13 lines of business (Tables 5 and 6). The

BRM subdivides the lines of business into 72 sub-functions. The *support delivery of services* and *management of resource* business areas are common to most Federal government agencies, and the information associated with each of their sub-functions is identified in this guideline as a *management and support* information type. Four additional *management and support* sub-factor information types have been defined to address privacy information. One additional *management and support* sub-factor information type has been defined to address General Information as a catch-all information type that may not be defined by the FEA BRM. As such, agencies may find it necessary to identify additional information types not defined in the BRM and assign associated security impact levels to those types.

4.1.2.1 Services Delivery Support Information

Most information systems employed in both service delivery support and resource management activities engage in one or more of the eight *support delivery of services* lines of business. Each of the information types associated with *support delivery of services* sub-functions is provided in Table 5. Volume II, Appendix C.2, "Services Delivery Support Functions," recommends provisional impact levels for confidentiality, integrity, and availability security objectives. These service support functions are the day-to-day activities necessary to provide the critical policy, programmatic, and managerial foundation that support Federal government operations. The direct service missions and constituencies ultimately being supported by service support functions comprise a significant factor in determining the security impacts associated with compromise of information associated with the *support delivery of services* business area.

Table 5: Services Delivery Support Functions and Information Types[15]

C.2.1 Controls and Oversight	C.2.4 Internal Risk Management & Mitigation	C.2.8 General Government
Corrective Action (Policy/Regulation)		Central Fiscal Operations
Program Evaluation	Contingency Planning	Legislative Functions
Program Monitoring	Continuity of Operations	Executive Functions
C.2.2 Regulatory Development	Service Recovery	Central Property Management
Policy & Guidance Development	**C.2.5 Revenue Collection**	Central Personnel Management
Public Comment Tracking	Debt Collection	Taxation Management
Regulatory Creation	User Fee Collection	Central Records & Statistics
Rule Publication	Federal Asset Sales	Management
C.2.3 Planning & Budgeting	**C.2.6 Public Affairs**	*Income Information*
Budget Formulation	Customer Services	*Personal Identity and Authentication*
Capital Planning	Official Information Dissemination	*Entitlement Event Information*
Enterprise Architecture	Product Outreach	*Representative Payee Information*
Strategic Planning	Public Relations	*General Information*
Budget Execution	**C.2.7 Legislative Relations**	
Workforce Planning	Legislation Tracking	
Management Improvement	Legislation Testimony	
Budgeting & Performance Integration	Proposal Development	
Tax & Fiscal Policy	Congressional Liaison Operations	

4.1.2.2 Government Resource Management Information

The *government resource management information* business area includes the back office support activities enabling the Federal government to operate effectively. The five *government resource management information* lines of business and the sub-functions associated with each

---

[15] The recommended information types provided in NIST SP 800-60 are established from the "business areas" and "lines of business" from OMB's Business Reference Model (BRM) section of Federal Enterprise Architecture (FEA) Consolidated Reference Model Document Version 2.3, October 2007.

information type are identified in Table 6. Volume II, Appendix C.3, "Government Resource Management Information," recommends provisional impact levels for confidentiality, integrity, and availability security objectives. Many departments and agencies operate their own support systems. Others obtain at least some support services from other organizations. Some agencies' missions are primarily to support other government departments and agencies in the conduct of direct service missions. As indicated above, security objectives and associated security impact levels for administrative and management information and systems are determined by the nature of the supported direct services and constituencies being supported.

Table 6: Government Resource Management Functions and Information Types[16]

C.3.1 Administrative Management	C.3.3 Human Resource Management	C.3.5 Information & Technology Management
Facilities, Fleet, and Equipment Management	HR Strategy	System Development
Help Desk Services	Staff Acquisition	Lifecycle/Change Management
Security Management	Organization & Position Mgmt	System Maintenance
Travel	Compensation Management	IT Infrastructure Maintenance
Workplace Policy Development & Management	Benefits Management	Information Security
C.3.2 Financial Management	Employee Performance Mgmt	Record Retention
Accounting	Employee Relations	Information Management
Funds Control	Labor Relations	System and Network Monitoring
Payments	Separation Management	Information Sharing
Collections and Receivables	Human Resources Development	
Asset and Liability Management	**C.3.4 Supply Chain Management**	
Reporting and Information	Goods Acquisition	
Cost Accounting/ Performance Measurement	Inventory Control	
	Logistics Management	
	Services Acquisition	

4.1.3 Legislative and Executive Information Mandates

During the identification of information types within an information system, agency personnel should afford special consideration for applicable governances addressing the information processed and the agency's supported mission. Volume II, Appendix E lists legislative and executive mandates establishing sensitivity and criticality guidelines for specific information types.

4.1.4 Identifying Information Types Not Listed in this Guideline

The FEA BRM Information Types are provided only as a taxonomy guideline. Not all information processed by an information system may be identified from Tables 4 through 6. Therefore, an agency may identify unique information types not listed in this guideline or may choose not to select provisional impact levels from Volume II, Appendix C (for management and support information types) or Volume II, Appendix D (for mission-based information types). Sections 4.2.1 through 4.2.3 of this guideline provide assistance to agencies in assigning provisional security categories to agency-identified information types and information systems.

Additionally, SP 800-60 provides a *management and support* sub function, General Information Type, which can be used by agencies as a means to identify and categorize information not

---

[16] The recommended information types provided in NIST SP 800-60 are established from the "business areas" and "lines of business" from OMB's Business Reference Model (BRM) section of Federal Enterprise Architecture (FEA) Consolidated Reference Model Document Version 2.3, October 2007.

contained in the FEA BRM. A complete description of the General Information Type information should be captured in the agency's collection and documentation process.

4.2 Step 2: Select Provisional Impact Level

In Step 2, organizations should establish provisional impact levels[17] based on the identified information types in Step 1. The provisional impact levels are the original impact levels assigned to the confidentiality, integrity, and availability security objectives of an information type from Volume II before any adjustments are made. Also in this step, the initial security categorization for the information type is established and documented.

Volume II, Appendix C suggests provisional confidentiality, integrity, and availability impact levels for management and support information types, and Volume II, Appendix D provides examples of provisional impact level assignments for mission-based information types. Using the impact assessment criteria identified in Section 3.2 for the security objectives and types of potential losses identified in Section 3.1.2, the organizational entity responsible for impact determination must assign impact levels and consequent security categorization for the *mission-based* and *management and support* information types identified for each information system.

4.2.1 FIPS 199 Security Categorization Criteria

Where an information type processed by an information system is not categorized by this guideline [based on information types identified in Volume II, Appendices C and D], an initial impact determination will need to be made based on FIPS 199 categorization criteria (cited in Table 7).

Agencies can assign security categories to information types and information systems by selecting and adjusting appropriate Table 7 values for the potential impact of compromises of confidentiality, integrity, and availability security objectives. Those responsible for impact level selection and subsequent security categorization should apply the criteria provided in Table 7 to each information type received by, processed in, stored in, and/or generated by each system for which they are responsible. The security categorization will generally be determined based on the most sensitive or critical information received by, processed in, stored in, and/or generated by the system under review.

---

[17] Impact levels (plural), as used here, refers to *low*, *moderate*, *high*, or *not applicable* values assigned to each security objective (i.e., confidentiality, integrity, and availability) used in expressing the security category of an information type or information systems. The value of *not applicable* only applies to information types and not to information systems.

Table 7: Categorization of Federal Information and Information Systems

SECURITY OBJECTIVE	POTENTIAL IMPACT		
	LOW	MODERATE	HIGH
Confidentiality Preserving authorized restrictions on information access and disclosure, including means for protecting personal privacy and proprietary information. [44 U.S.C., SEC. 3542]	The unauthorized disclosure of information could be expected to have a **limited** adverse effect on organizational operations, organizational assets, or individuals.	The unauthorized disclosure of information could be expected to have a **serious** adverse effect on organizational operations, organizational assets, or individuals.	The unauthorized disclosure of information could be expected to have a **severe or catastrophic** adverse effect on organizational operations, organizational assets, or individuals.
Integrity Guarding against improper information modification or destruction, and includes ensuring information non-repudiation and authenticity. [44 U.S.C., SEC. 3542]	The unauthorized modification or destruction of information could be expected to have a **limited** adverse effect on organizational operations, organizational assets, or individuals.	The unauthorized modification or destruction of information could be expected to have a **serious** adverse effect on organizational operations, organizational assets, or individuals.	The unauthorized modification or destruction of information could be expected to have a **severe or catastrophic** adverse effect on organizational operations, organizational assets, or individuals.
Availability Ensuring timely and reliable access to and use of information. [44 U.S.C., SEC. 3542]	The disruption of access to or use of information or an information system could be expected to have a **limited** adverse effect on organizational operations, organizational assets, or individuals.	The disruption of access to or use of information or an information system could be expected to have a **serious** adverse effect on organizational operations, organizational assets, or individuals.	The disruption of access to or use of information or an information system could be expected to have a **severe or catastrophic** adverse effect on organizational operations, organizational assets, or individuals.

4.2.2 Common Factors for Selection of Impact Levels

Where an agency determines security impact levels and security categorization based on local application of FIPS 199 criteria, it is recommended that the following factors be considered with respect to security impacts for each information type.

4.2.2.1 Confidentiality Factors

Using the FIPS 199 potential impact criteria summarized in Table 7, each information type should be evaluated for confidentiality with respect to the impact level associated with unauthorized disclosure of (i) each known variant of the information belonging to the type and (ii) each use of the information by the system under review. Answers to the following questions will help in the evaluation process:

- How can a malicious adversary use the unauthorized disclosure of information to do limited/serious/severe harm to agency operations, agency assets, or individuals?

- How can a malicious adversary use the unauthorized disclosure of information to gain control of agency assets that might result in unauthorized modification of information, destruction of information, or denial of system services that would result in limited/serious/severe harm to agency operations, agency assets, or individuals?

20

- Would unauthorized disclosure/dissemination of elements of the information type violate laws, executive orders, or agency regulations?

4.2.2.2   Integrity Factors

Using the FIPS 199 potential impact criteria summarized in Table 7, each information type should be evaluated for integrity with respect to the impact level associated with unauthorized modification or destruction of (i) each known variant of the information belonging to the type and (ii) each use of the information by the system under review. Answers to the following questions will help in the evaluation process:

- How can a malicious adversary use the unauthorized modification or destruction of information to do limited/serious/severe harm to agency operations, agency assets, or individuals?

- Would unauthorized modification/destruction of elements of the information type violate laws, executive orders, or agency regulations?

Unauthorized modification or destruction of information can take many forms. The changes can be subtle and hard to detect, or they can occur on a massive scale. One can construct an extraordinarily wide range of scenarios for modification of information and its likely consequences. Just a few examples include forging or modifying information to:

- Reduce public confidence in an agency;

- Fraudulently achieve financial gain;

- Create confusion or controversy by promulgating a fraudulent or incorrect procedure;

- Initiate confusion or controversy through false attribution of a fraudulent or false policy;

- Influence personnel decisions;

- Interfere with or manipulate law enforcement or legal processes;

- Influence legislation; or

- Achieve unauthorized access to government information or facilities.

In most cases, the most serious impacts of integrity compromise occur when some action is taken that is based on the modified information or the modified information is disseminated to other organizations or the public.

Undetected loss of integrity can be catastrophic for many information types. The consequences of integrity compromise can be either direct (e.g., modification of a financial entry, medical alert, or criminal record) or indirect (e.g., facilitation of unauthorized access to sensitive or private information or deny access to information or information system services). Malicious use of write access to information and information systems can do enormous harm to an agency's mission and can be employed to use an agency system as a proxy for attacks on other systems.

In many cases, the consequences of unauthorized modification or destruction of information to agency mission functions and public confidence in the agency can be expected to be limited. In other cases, integrity compromises can result in the endangerment of human life or other severe consequences. The impact can be particularly severe in the case of time-critical information.

4.2.2.3 Availability Factors

Using the FIPS 199 potential impact criteria summarized in Table 7, each information type should be evaluated for availability with respect to the impact level associated with the disruption of access to or use of information of (i) each known variant of the information belonging to the type and (ii) each use of the information by the system under review. Answers to the following questions will help in the evaluation process:

- How can a malicious adversary use the disruption of access to or use of information to do limited/serious/severe harm to agency operations, agency assets, or individuals?

- Would disruption of access to or use of elements of the information type violate laws, executive orders, or agency regulations?

For many information types and information systems, the availability impact level depends on how long the information or system remains unavailable. Undetected loss of availability can be catastrophic for many information types. For example, permanent loss of budget execution, contingency planning, continuity of operations, service recovery, debt collection, taxation management, personnel management, payroll management, security management, inventory control, logistics management, or accounting information databases would be catastrophic for almost any agency. Complete reconstruction of such databases would be time consuming and expensive.

In most cases, the adverse effects of a limited-duration availability compromise on an organization's mission functions and public confidence will be limited. In contrast, for time-critical information types, availability is less likely to be restored before serious harm is done to agency assets, operations, or personnel (or to public welfare). In such instances, the documented availability impact level recommendations should indicate the information is time-critical and the basis for criticality.

4.2.3 Examples of FIPS 199-Based Selection of Impact Levels

FIPS 199-based examples of security objective impact selection and security categorization for sample information types follow:

EXAMPLE 1: An organization managing *public information* on its web server determines that there is no potential impact from a loss of confidentiality (i.e., confidentiality requirements are not applicable), a moderate potential impact from a loss of integrity, and a moderate potential impact from a loss of availability. The resulting security category of this information type is expressed as:

> Security Category $_{\text{public information}}$ = {(confidentiality, n/a), (integrity, moderate), (availability, moderate)}.

EXAMPLE 2: A law enforcement organization managing extremely sensitive *investigative information* determines that the potential impact from a loss of confidentiality is high, the potential impact from a loss of integrity is moderate, and the potential impact from a loss of availability is moderate. The resulting security category for this type of information is expressed as:

Security Category $_{\text{investigative information}}$ = {(confidentiality, high), (integrity, moderate), (availability, moderate)}.

EXAMPLE 3: A financial organization managing routine *administrative information* (not privacy-related information) determines that the potential impact from a loss of confidentiality is low, the potential impact from a loss of integrity is low, and the potential impact from a loss of availability is low. The resulting security category of this information type is expressed as:

Security Category $_{\text{administrative information}}$ = {(confidentiality, low), (integrity, low), (availability, low)}.

In general, security objective impact assessment is independent of mechanisms employed to mitigate the consequences of a compromise.

4.3 Step 3: Review Provisional Impact Levels and Adjust/Finalize Information Type Impact Levels

In Step 3, organizations should review and adjust the provisional security impact levels for the security objectives of each information type and arrive at a finalized state. To accomplish this, organizations should: (i) review the appropriateness of the provisional impact levels based on the organization, environment, mission, use, and data sharing; (ii) adjust the security objective impact levels as necessary using the special factors[18] guidance found in Volume II, Appendices C and D; and (iii) document all adjustments to the impact levels and provide the rationale or justification for the adjustments.

When security categorization impact levels recommended in Section 4.2 or Volume II, Appendices C and D are adopted as provisional security impact levels, the agency should review the appropriateness of the provisional impact levels in the context of the organization, environment, mission, use, and data sharing associated with the information system under review. This review should include the agency's mission importance; lifecycle and timeliness implications; configuration and security policy related information; special handling requirements; etc. The FIPS 199 factors presented in Section 4.2.2 of this document should be used as the basis for decisions regarding adjustment or finalization of the provisional impact levels. The confidentiality, integrity, and availability impact levels may be adjusted one or more times in the course of the review. Once the review and adjustment process is complete, the mapping of impact levels by information type can be finalized.

The impact of information compromise of a particular type can vary in different agencies or in dissimilar operational contexts. Also, the impact for an information type may vary throughout the life cycle. For example, contract information that has a *moderate* confidentiality impact level during the life of the contract may have a *low* impact level when the contract is completed. Policy information may have *moderate* confidentiality and integrity impact levels during the policy development process, *low* confidentiality and *moderate* integrity impact levels when the policy is implemented, and *low* confidentiality and integrity impact levels when the policy is no longer used.

---

[18] The special factor guidance in NIST SP 800-60, Volume II, provides specific guidance on considerations for adjusting each security objective (confidentiality, integrity, and availability) for each information type. The special factor guidance is applied to each information type, based on how the information type is used, the organization's mission, or the system's operating environment.

The impact levels associated with the *management and support* information common to many agencies are strongly affected by the *mission-based* information with which it is associated. That is, agency-common management and support information used with very sensitive or critical mission-based information types may have higher impact levels than the same agency-common information used with less critical mission-based information types.

Further, information systems process many types of information. Not all of these information types are likely to have the same security impact levels. The compromise of some information types will jeopardize system functionality and agency mission more than the compromise of other information types. System security impact levels must be assessed in the context of system mission and function as well as on the basis of the aggregate of the component information types.

Additionally, configuration and security policy enforcement information should be reviewed and adjusted considering the information processed on the system. Configuration and security policy information includes password files, network access rules, other hardware and software configuration settings, and documentation affecting access to the information system's data, programs, and/or processes. At a minimum, a low confidentiality and integrity impact level will apply to this set of information and processes due to a potential for corruption, misuse, or abuse of system information and processes.

A factor specific to the confidentiality objective is information subject to special handling (e.g., information subject to the Privacy Act of 1974, 5 U.S.C. § 552A). Regardless of other considerations, some minimum confidentiality impact level must be assigned to any information system that stores, processes, or generates such information. Examples of such information include information subject to the Trade Secrets Act, the Privacy Act, Department of Energy Safeguards Information, Internal Revenue Service Official Use Only Information, and Environmental Protection Agency Confidential Business Information (e.g., subject to Toxic Substances Control Act; Resource Conservation and Recovery Act; Comprehensive Environmental Response, Compensation, and Liability Act). Some of these statutory and regulatory specifications are listed in Volume II, Appendix E, "Legislative and Executive Sources Establishing Sensitivity/Criticality."

4.4 Step 4: Assign System Security Category

Once the security impact levels have been selected, reviewed and adjusted as necessary for the security objectives of each individual information type processed by an information system, it is necessary to assign a system security category based on the aggregate of information types. The Step 4 activities include the following: (i) review identified security categorizations for the aggregate of information types; (ii) determine the system security categorization by identifying the high water mark for each of the security objectives (confidentiality, integrity, availability) based on the aggregate of the information types; (iii) adjust the high water mark for each system security objective, as necessary, by applying the factors discussed in section 4.4.2; (iv) assign the overall information system impact level based on the highest impact level for the system security objectives; and (v) document all security categorization determinations and decisions.

4.4.1 FIPS 199 Process for System Security Categorization

FIPS 199 recognizes that determining the security category of an information system requires additional analysis and must consider the security categories of all information types resident on the information system. For an information system, the potential security impact levels assigned to each of the respective security objectives (confidentiality, integrity, availability) are the highest level (i.e., high water mark) for any one of these objectives that has been determined for the types of information resident on the information system.

Information systems are composed of both computer programs and information. Programs in execution within an information system (i.e., system processes) facilitate the processing, storage, and transmission of information and are necessary for the organization to conduct its essential business functions and operations. These system-processing functions also require protection and could be subject to security categorization as well. However, in the interest of simplification, it is assumed that the security categorization of all information types associated with the information system provide an appropriate worst case potential for the overall information system—thereby obviating the need to consider the system processes in the security categorization of the information system. This is in recognition of:

- The fundamental requirement to protect the integrity, availability, and, for key information such as passwords and encryption keys, the confidentiality of system-level processing functions and information at the high water mark; and

- The strong interdependence between confidentiality, integrity, and availability.

For this reason, FIPS 199 notes that, while the value (i.e., level) of *not applicable* can apply to a security objective for specific information types processed by systems, this value cannot be assigned to any security objective for an information system. There is a minimum provisional impact (i.e., low water mark) for a compromise of confidentiality, integrity, and availability for an information system. This is necessary to protect the system-level processing functions and information critical to the operation of the information system.

The generalized format for expressing the security category, or *SC*, of an information system is:

$$SC_{\text{information system}} = \{(\text{confidentiality}, \textit{impact}), (\text{integrity}, \textit{impact}), (\text{availability}, \textit{impact})\},$$

where the acceptable values for potential impact are LOW, MODERATE, or HIGH.

The following examples illustrate the system security categorization process described in FIPS 199.

SYSTEM EXAMPLE 1: An information system used for large acquisitions in a contracting organization contains both sensitive, pre-solicitation phase contract information and routine administrative information. The management within the contracting organization determines that: (i) for the sensitive contract information, the potential impact from a loss of confidentiality is moderate, the potential impact from a loss of integrity is moderate, and the potential impact from a loss of availability is low; and (ii) for the routine administrative information (non-privacy-related information), the potential impact from a loss of confidentiality is low, the potential impact from a loss of integrity is low, and the potential impact from a loss of availability is low. The resulting security categories, or *SC*, of these information types are expressed as:

SC $_{\text{contract information}}$ = {(confidentiality, MODERATE), (integrity, MODERATE), (availability, LOW)}, and

SC $_{\text{administrative information}}$ = {(confidentiality, LOW), (integrity, LOW), (availability, LOW)}.

The resulting security category of the information system is expressed as:

SC $_{\text{acquisition system}}$ = {(confidentiality, MODERATE), (integrity, MODERATE), (availability, LOW)},

representing the high water mark or maximum potential impact values for each security objective from the information types resident on the acquisition system.

SYSTEM EXAMPLE 2: A power plant contains a SCADA (supervisory control and data acquisition) system controlling the distribution f electric power for a large military installation. The SCADA system contains both real-time sensor data and routine administrative information. The management at the power plant determines that: (i) for the sensor data being acquired by the SCADA system, there is no potential impact from a loss of confidentiality, a high potential impact from a loss of integrity, and a high potential impact from a loss of availability; and (ii) for the administrative information being processed by the system, there is a low potential impact from a loss of confidentiality, a low potential impact from a loss of integrity, and a low potential impact from a loss of availability. The resulting security categories, or *SC*, of these information types are expressed as:

SC $_{\text{sensor data}}$ = {(confidentiality, NA), (integrity, HIGH), (availability, HIGH)}, and

SC $_{\text{administrative information}}$ = {(confidentiality, LOW), (integrity, LOW), (availability, LOW)}.

The resulting security category of the information system is initially expressed as:

SC $_{\text{SCADA system}}$ = {(confidentiality, LOW), (integrity, HIGH), (availability, HIGH)},

representing the high water mark or maximum potential impact values for each security objective from the information types resident on the SCADA system. The management at the power plant chooses to increase the potential impact from a loss of confidentiality from low to moderate reflecting a more realistic view of the potential impact on the information system should there be a security breach due to the unauthorized disclosure of system-level information or processing functions. The final security category of the information system is expressed as:

SC $_{\text{SCADA system}}$ = {(confidentiality, MODERATE), (integrity, HIGH), (availability, HIGH)}.

4.4.2 Guidelines for System Categorization

In some cases, the impact level for a system security category will be higher than any security objective impact level for any information type processed by the system.

The primary factors that most commonly raise the impact levels of the system security category above that of its constituent information types are aggregation and critical system functionality. Additionally, variations in sensitivity/criticality with respect to time may need to be factored into the impact assignment process. Some information loses its sensitivity in time (e.g., economic/commodity projections after they've been published). Other information is particularly critical at some point in time (e.g., weather data in the terminal approach area during aircraft landing operations). This section provides some general guidelines regarding how aggregation, critical functionality, and other system factors may affect system security categorization.

In order to effectively accomplish this step, various stakeholders (e.g., management, operational personnel, or security experts) may need to be involved in decisions regarding system-level impact assessments. The following sections provide factors to consider in adjusting the system security objective impact levels.

4.4.2.1 Aggregation

Some information may have little or no sensitivity in isolation but may be highly sensitive in aggregation. In some cases, aggregation of large quantities of a single information type can reveal sensitive patterns and plans, or facilitate access to sensitive or critical systems. In other cases, aggregation of information of several different and seemingly innocuous types can have similar effects. In general, the sensitivity of a given data element is likely to be greater in context than in isolation (e.g., association of an account number with the identity of an individual and/or institution). The availability, routine operational employment, and sophistication of data aggregation and inference tools are all increasing rapidly. If review reveals increased sensitivity or criticality associated with information aggregates, then the system security objective impact levels may need to be adjusted to a higher level than would be indicated by the security impact levels associated with any individual information type. This could be implemented by incorporating a statement that explains the aggregation and potential security objective affected as well as the modification to impact levels.

4.4.2.2 Critical System Functionality

Compromise of some information types may have low impact in the context of a system's primary function but may have much more significance when viewed in the context of the potential impact of compromising:

- Other systems to which the system in question is connected, or

- Other systems which are dependent on that system's information.

Access control information for a system that processes only low impact information might initially be thought to have only low impact security objectives. However, if access to that system might result in some form of access to other systems (e.g., over a network), the sensitivity and criticality attributes of all systems to which such indirect access can result needs to be considered. Similarly, some information may, in general, have low sensitivity and/or criticality security objectives. However, that information may be used by other systems to enable extremely sensitive or critical functions (e.g., air traffic control use of weather information or use of commercial flight information to identify military combat transport systems). Loss of data integrity, availability, temporal context, or other context can have catastrophic consequences.

4.4.2.3   Extenuating Circumstances

This publication focuses on categorizing an information system based on its information types and associated security objective impacts. There are times when a system security objective impact level should be elevated based on reasons other than its information. For example, the information system provides critical process flow or security capability, the visibility of the system to the public, the sheer number of other systems reliant on its operation or possibly its overall cost of replacement. These examples, given a specific situation, may provide reason for the system owner to increase the overall security impact level of a system.

An elevation based on extenuating circumstances can be more apparent by comparing the original security categorization to the business impact analysis. If the system was categorized based on FIPS 199 at a Moderate overall impact level but the system owner has determined it needs to be operational within 4-8 hours of a disruption irrespective of the aggregated information type availability security impact level assigned, then there is a disconnect that might be caused by the system's extenuating circumstances. Agencies must customize the information system availability security impact level as appropriate to obtain full value and accuracy.

4.4.2.4   Other System Factors

Public Information Integrity

Most Federal agencies maintain web pages that are accessible to the public. The vast majority of these public web pages permit interaction between the site and the public. In some cases, the site provides only information. In other cases, forms may be submitted via the website (e.g., applications for service or job applications). In some cases, the site is a medium for business transactions. Unauthorized modification or destruction of information affecting external communications (e.g., web pages, electronic mail) may adversely affect operations and/or public confidence in the agency. In most cases, the damage can be corrected within a relatively short period of time, and the damage is limited (impact level is *low*). In other cases (e.g., very large fraudulent transactions or modification of a web page belonging to an intelligence/security community component), the damage to mission function and/or public confidence in the agency can be serious. In such cases, the integrity impact associated with unauthorized modification or destruction of a public web page would be at least *moderate.*

Catastrophic Loss of System Availability

Either physical or logical destruction of major assets can result in very large expenditures to restore the assets and/or long periods of time for recovery. Permanent loss/unavailability of information system capabilities can seriously hamper agency operations and, where direct services to the public are involved, have a severe adverse effect on public confidence in Federal agencies. Particularly in the case of large systems, FIPS 199 criteria suggest that catastrophic loss of system availability may result in a *high* availability impact level. Whether or not the impact level of system availability should be *high* (and subsequent *high* system security impact level) is dependent on other factors, such as cost and criticality of the system, rather than on the security impact levels for the information types being processed by the system.

Large Supporting and Interconnecting Systems

Large or complex information systems composed of multiple lower level systems often require additional consideration regarding assignment of system security categorization. This section will provide guidelines for applying and interrelating individual system security categorization results to enterprise organizations, large supporting infrastructures (such as general support systems, data warehouse applications, large data storage units, server farms, and information repositories), and interconnecting systems.

Upon security categorization identification for all information systems interacting with large infrastructure systems, senior IT and security officials have possession of valuable information that can now enable an enterprise wide security perspective. One significant activity includes levying an overall security categorization for the agency's supporting network infrastructures. Since networks, as well as other general support systems, do not inherently "own" mission-based or management and support information types, the infrastructure's categorization is based on the aggregation of the information systems' security categorizations. In other words, the infrastructure's security categorization is the high water mark of the supported information systems and is based on the information types processed, flowed, or stored on the network or general support system. Together, the top down enterprise wide threat assessment and bottom up security assessment derived by aggregation will allow an organization to look at its risk profile from a comprehensive and balanced view. Further, this analysis will ensure the proper application of common security controls supporting the multiple information systems and the protection provided by those controls are inherited by the individual systems.

Critical Infrastructures and Key Resources

Where the mission served by an information system, or the information that the system processes, affects the security of critical infrastructures and key resources, the harm that results from a compromise requires particularly close attention. In this case, an effect on security might include a significant reduction in the effectiveness of physical or cyber security protection mechanisms, or facilitation of a terrorist attack on critical infrastructures and key resources. Accordingly, the system security categorization should be carefully determined when a loss of confidentiality, integrity, or availability will result in a negative impact on the critical infrastructures and key resources.

The *Critical Information Infrastructure Act of 2002*, Public Law 107-296 §§ 211-215 of November 25, 2002 (codified as 6 U.S.C. 131-134), defines the term "critical infrastructure information" to mean information not customarily in the public domain and related to the security of critical infrastructure or protected systems. Should information types be aligned with Critical Infrastructures, then action should be taken to ensure compliance with Homeland Security Presidential Directive No. 7 (HSPD 7) and to initiate an interdependency analysis.

Privacy Information

The *E-Government Act of 2002* complements privacy protection requirements of the *Privacy Act of 1974*. Under the terms of these public laws, Federal government agencies have specific responsibilities regarding collection, dissemination or disclosure of information regarding individuals.[19]

The September 26, 2003 OMB Memorandum M-03-22, "OMB Guidance for Implementing the Privacy Provisions of the E-Government Act of 2002," puts the privacy provisions of the E-Government Act of 2002 into effect. The guidance applies to information that identifies individuals in a recognizable form, including name, address, telephone number, Social Security Number, and e-mail addresses. OMB instructed agency heads "to describe how the government handles information that individuals provide electronically, so that the American public has assurances that personal information is protected." Under these public laws and executive policies, it is necessary to broaden the definition of "unauthorized disclosure" to encompass *any* access, use, disclosure, or sharing of privacy-protected information among Federal government agencies when such actions are prohibited by privacy laws and policies. Since most privacy regulations focus on access, use, disclosure, or sharing of information, privacy considerations are dealt with in this guideline as special factors affecting the confidentiality impact level. In establishing confidentiality impact levels for each information type, responsible parties must consider the consequences of unauthorized disclosure of privacy information (with respect to violations of Federal policy and/or law).

Agencies are required to conduct Privacy Impact Assessments (PIAs) before developing IT systems that contain personally identifiable information or before collecting personally identifiable information electronically. The impact of privacy violations should consider any adverse effects experienced by individuals or organizations as a result of the loss of PII confidentiality. Examples of adverse effects experienced by individuals may include blackmail, identity theft, discrimination, or emotional distress. Examples of adverse effects experienced by organizations may include administrative burden, financial losses, loss of public reputation and confidence, and the penalties associated with violation of the relevant statutes and policies.

Categorizations should be reviewed to ensure that the adverse effects of a loss of PII confidentiality have been adequately factored into impact determinations. The confidentiality impact level should generally fall into the ***moderate*** range.

Trade Secrets

There are several laws that specifically prohibit unauthorized disclosure of trade secrets (e.g., 7 U.S.C., Chapter 6, Subchapter II, Section 136h and 42 U.S.C., Chapter 6A, Subchapter XII, Part E, Section 300j-4(d)(1)). Systems that store, communicate, or process trade secrets will generally be assigned at least a ***moderate*** confidentiality impact level.

4.4.3 Overall Information System Impact

Since the impact values (i.e., levels) for confidentiality, integrity, and availability may not always be the same for a particular information system, the high water mark concept[20] is used to

---

[19] The OMB definition of an individual is, "a citizen of the United States or an alien lawfully admitted for permanent residence." Agencies may choose to extend the protections of the Privacy Act and E-Government Act to businesses, sole proprietors, aliens, etc.

determine the overall impact level of the information system. The security impact level for an information system will generally be the highest impact level for the security objectives (confidentiality, integrity, and availability) associated with the aggregate of system information types. Thus, a low-impact system is defined as an information system in which all three of the security objectives are low. A moderate-impact system is an information system in which at least one of the security objectives is moderate and no security objective is greater than moderate. And finally, a high-impact system is an information system in which at least one security objective is high.

4.5 Documenting the Security Categorization Process

Essential to the security categorization process is documenting the research, key decisions and approvals, and supporting rationale driving the information system security categorization. This information is key to supporting the security life cycle and will need to be included in the information system's security plan.

Figure 3 provides an example of information details that should be collected.

---

[20] The high water mark concept is employed because there are significant dependencies among the security objectives of confidentiality, integrity, and availability. In most cases, a compromise in one security objective ultimately affects the other security objectives as well.

Information System Name: SCADA System [and Agency specific identifier]		
Business and Mission Supported: The SCADA (supervisory control and data acquisition) system provides real-time control and information supporting the main power plant. The power plant provides critical distribution of electric power to the military installation.		
Information Types		
[D.7.1] Energy Supply	Sensor data monitoring the availability of energy for the Military installation and its soldiers and command authority. This function includes control of distribution and transfer of power. The SCADA remote control capabilities can take action such as initiating necessary switching actions to alleviate an overloading power condition. The impacts to this information and the SCADA system may affect the installation's critical infrastructures.	
[C.2.8.12]General Information	The SCADA information system processes routine administrative information.	

Step 1 Identify Information Types	Step 2 [Provisional] / Step 3a [Adjustments]		
	Confidentiality Impact	Integrity Impact	Availability Impact
	Step 3b- Impact Adjustment Justification		
Energy Supply	L / M	L / H	L / H
	Disclosure of sensor information may seriously impact the missions if indications & warnings of overall capability are provided to an adversary.	Severe impacts or consequences may occur if adversarial modification of information results in incorrect power system regulation or control actions.	Due to loss of availability, severe impact to the mission capability may result and may in-turn have overall catastrophic consequences for the facility's critical infrastructures and possible loss of human life.
General Information	L	L	L
	No adjustments	No adjustments	No adjustments
Step 4 System Categorization:	Moderate	High	High
	Overall Information System Impact: High		

Figure 3: Security Categorization Information Collection

In addition, agencies may consider enhancing their SSPs with other analyses, decisions, assignments, and or approvals that were used in the categorization process. Examples may include:

- Agency's business and mission areas (Step 1 in Table 1)

- Legislative and executive information mandates affecting the information impact assignment or adjustment (Section 4.1.3)

- Indicating whether the information is time-critical in rationales for assigning availability impact levels (Section 4.2.2.3)

- Rationales for assigning information to the General Information Type (Section 4.1.2, Implementation Tip)

- Results of reviews of the appropriateness of the provisional impact levels for information (Section 4.3)

- Results of considering the potential impacts to other organizations and considering, "in accordance with the USA Patriot Act of 2001 and Homeland Security Presidential Directives, potential national-level impacts in categorizing the information system" (NIST SP 800-53 security control RA-2)

- Results of reviewing the identified security categorizations for the aggregate of information types (Step 4 in Table 1)

- Effects of various factors and circumstances (e.g., data aggregation, critical system functionality, privacy, trade secrets, critical infrastructure, aggregation, critical system functionality, extenuating circumstances) on the system category (Section 4.4.2)

- Whether and why the agency determined that the system impact level must be higher than any of the levels of the information types that the system processes (Section 4.4)

- Approvals of all determinations or decisions (Step 4 in Table 1)

4.6 Uses of Categorization Information

The results of system security categorization can and should be used by, or made available to, appropriate agency personnel to support agency activities including:

- Business Impact Analysis (BIA): Agency personnel should consider the cross-utilization of security categorization and BIA information in the performance of each activity. Their common objectives enable agencies to mutually draw from them, thus, providing checks and balances to ensure accuracy for each information system. Conflicting information and anomalous conditions, such as a low availability impact and a BIA three-hour recovery time objective, should trigger a reevaluation by the mission and data owners.

- Capital Planning and Investment Control (CPIC) and Enterprise Architecture (EA): Just as no IT investment should be made without a business-approved architecture,[21] the security categorization that begins the security life cycle is a business-enabling activity directly feeding the enterprise architecture and CPIC processes for new investments, as well as migration and upgrade decisions. Specifically, the security categorization can provide a firm basis for justifying certain capital expenditures and also can provide analytical input to avoid unnecessary investments.

- System Design: Understanding and designing the system architecture with varying information sensitivity levels in mind may assist in achieving economies of scale with security services and protection through common security zones within the enterprise. For example, an information system containing privacy information may be located in one security zone with other information systems containing similar sensitive information. Each zone may have varying levels of security. For instance, the more critical zones may require 3-factor authentication where the open area may only require normal access controls. This type of approach requires a solid understanding of an agency's information and data types gained through the security categorization process.

---

[21] FEA Consolidated Reference Model Document Version 2.3, October 2007

- Contingency and Disaster Recovery Planning: Contingency and disaster recovery planning personnel should review information systems that have multiple data types of varying impact levels and consider grouping applications with similar information system impact levels with sufficiently protected infrastructures. This ensures efficient application of the correct contingency and disaster protection security controls and avoids the over protection of lower impact information systems.

- Information Sharing and System Interconnection Agreements: Agency personnel should utilize aggregated and individual security categorization information when assessing interagency connections. For example, knowing that information processed on a high impact information system is flowing to another agency's moderate impact information system should cause both agencies to evaluate the security categorization information, the implemented or resulting security controls, and the risk associated with interconnecting systems. The results of this evaluation may substantiate the need for additional security controls in the form of a Service Level Agreement, information systems upgrades, additional mitigating security controls, or alternative means of sharing the required information.

APPENDIX A: GLOSSARY OF TERMS

Accreditation	The official management decision given by a senior agency official to authorize operation of an information system and to explicitly accept the risk to agency operations (including mission, functions, image, or reputation), agency assets, or individuals, based on the implementation of an agreed-upon set of security controls. [FIPS 200, NIST SP 800-37]
Accreditation Boundary	All components of an information system to be accredited by an authorizing official and excludes separately accredited systems to which the information system is connected. Synonymous with the term security perimeter defined in CNSS Instruction 4009 and DCID 6/3. [NIST SP 800-37]
Accrediting Authority	See Authorizing Official.
Agency	An executive department specified in 5 U.S.C., Sec. 101; a military department specified in 5 U.S.C., Sec. 102; an independent establishment as defined in 5 U.S.C., Sec. 104(1); and a wholly owned Government corporation fully subject to the provisions of 31 U.S.C., Chapter 91. [41 U.S.C., Sec. 403]
Authentication	Verifying the identity of a user, process, or device, often as a prerequisite to allowing access to resources in an information system. [FIPS 200]
Authenticity	The property of being genuine and being able to be verified and trusted; confidence in the validity of a transmission, a message, or message originator. See authentication.
Authorizing Official	Official with the authority to formally assume responsibility for operating an information system at an acceptable level of risk to agency operations (including mission, functions, image, or reputation), agency assets, or individuals. Synonymous with Accreditation Authority. [FIPS 200, NIST SP 800-37]
Availability	Ensuring timely and reliable access to and use of information. [44 U.S.C., Sec. 3542]

Business Areas	"Business areas" separate government operations into high-level categories relating to the purpose of government, the mechanisms the government uses to achieve its purposes, the support functions necessary to conduct government operations, and resource management functions that support all areas of the government's business. "Business areas" are subdivided into "areas of operation" or "lines of business." The recommended information types provided in NIST SP 800-60 are established from the "business areas" and "lines of business" from OMB's Business Reference Model (BRM) section of *Federal Enterprise Architecture (FEA) Consolidated Reference Model Document Version 2.3*
Certification	A comprehensive assessment of the management, operational, and technical security controls in an information system, made in support of security accreditation, to determine the extent to which the controls are implemented correctly, operating as intended, and producing the desired outcome with respect to meeting the security requirements for the system. [FIPS 200, NIST SP 800-37]
Chief Information Officer	Agency official responsible for: (i) Providing advice and other assistance to the head of the executive agency and other senior management personnel of the agency to ensure that information technology is acquired and information resources are managed in a manner that is consistent with laws, Executive Orders, directives, policies, regulations, and priorities established by the head of the agency; (ii) Developing, maintaining, and facilitating the implementation of a sound and integrated information technology architecture for the agency; and (iii) Promoting the effective and efficient design and operation of all major information resources management processes for the agency, including improvements to work processes of the agency. [PL 104-106, Sec. 5125(b)]
Classified Information	Information that has been determined pursuant to Executive Order (E.O.) 13292 or any predecessor order to require protection against unauthorized disclosure and is marked to indicate its classified status when in documentary form.

Command and Control	The exercise of authority and direction by a properly designated commander over assigned and attached forces in the accomplishment of the mission. Command and control functions are performed through an arrangement of personnel, equipment, communications, facilities, and procedures employed by a commander in planning, directing, coordinating, and controlling forces and operations in the accomplishment of the mission.
Confidentiality	Preserving authorized restrictions on information access and disclosure, including means for protecting personal privacy and proprietary information. [44 U.S.C., Sec. 3542]
Counterintelligence	Information gathered and activities conducted to protect against espionage, other intelligence activities, sabotage, or assassinations conducted by or on behalf of foreign governments or elements thereof, foreign organizations, or foreign persons, or international terrorist activities.
Criticality	A measure of the degree to which an organization depends on the information or information system for the success of a mission or of a business function.
Cryptologic	Of or pertaining to cryptology.
Cryptology	The science that deals with hidden, disguised, or encrypted communications. It includes communications security and communications intelligence.
Executive Agency	An executive department specified in 5 U.S.C., Sec. 101; a military department specified in 5 U.S.C., Sec.102; an independent establishment as defined in 5 U.S.C., Sec. 104(1); or a wholly owned government corporation fully subject to the provisions of 31 U.S.C., Chapter 91. [41 U.S.C., Sec. 403]
Federal Enterprise Architecture [FEA Program Management Office]	A business-based framework for government-wide improvement developed by the Office of Management and Budget that is intended to facilitate efforts to transform the federal government to one that is citizen-centered, results-oriented, and market-based.
Federal Information System	An information system used or operated by an executive agency, by a contractor of an executive agency, or by another organization on behalf of an executive agency. [40 U.S.C., Sec. 11331]

General Support System	An interconnected set of information resources under the same direct management control that shares common functionality. It normally includes hardware, software, information, data, applications, communications, and people. [OMB Circular A-130, Appendix III]
High-Impact System	An information system in which at least one security objective (i.e., confidentiality, integrity, or availability) is assigned a FIPS 199 potential impact value of high. [FIPS 200]
Impact	The magnitude of harm that can be expected to result from the consequences of unauthorized disclosure of information, unauthorized modification of information, unauthorized destruction of information, or loss of information or information system availability.
Independent Regulatory Agency	The Board of Governors of the Federal Reserve System, the Commodity Futures Trading Commission, the Consumer Product Safety Commission, the Federal Communications Commission, the Federal Deposit Insurance Corporation, the Federal Energy Regulatory Commission, the Federal Housing Finance Board, the Federal Maritime Commission, the Federal Trade Commission, the Interstate Commerce Commission, the Mine Enforcement Safety and Health Review Commission, the National Labor Relations Board, the Nuclear Regulatory Commission, the Occupational Safety and Health Review Commission, the Postal Rate Commission, the Securities and Exchange Commission, and any other similar agency designated by statute as a Federal independent regulatory agency or commission.
Individual	A citizen of the United States or an alien lawfully admitted for permanent residence. Agencies may, consistent with individual practice, choose to extend the protections of the Privacy Act and E-Government Act to businesses, sole proprietors, aliens, etc.
Information	An instance of an information type. [FIPS 199]
Information Owner	Official with statutory or operational authority for specified information and responsibility for establishing the controls for its generation, collection, processing, dissemination, and disposal. [CNSS Inst. 4009]
Information Resources	Information and related resources, such as personnel, equipment, funds, and information technology. [44 U.S.C., Sec. 3502]
Information Security	The protection of information and information systems from unauthorized access, use, disclosure, disruption, modification, or destruction in order to provide confidentiality, integrity, and availability. [44 U.S.C., Sec. 3542]

Information System	A discrete set of information resources organized for the collection, processing, maintenance, use, sharing, dissemination, or disposition of information. [44 U.S.C., Sec. 3502; OMB Circular A-130, Appendix III]
Information System Owner (or Program Manager)	Official responsible for the overall procurement, development, integration, modification, or operation and maintenance of an information system. [CNSS Inst. 4009, Adapted]
Information System Security Officer	Individual assigned responsibility by the senior agency information security officer, authorizing official, management official, or information system owner for maintaining the appropriate operational security posture for an information system or program. [CNSS Inst. 4009, Adapted]
Information Technology	Any equipment or interconnected system or subsystem of equipment that is used in the automatic acquisition, storage, manipulation, management, movement, control, display, switching, interchange, transmission, or reception of data or information by the executive agency. For purposes of the preceding sentence, equipment is used by an executive agency if the equipment is used by the executive agency directly or is used by a contractor under a contract with the executive agency which: (i) requires the use of such equipment; or (ii) requires the use, to a significant extent, of such equipment in the performance of a service or the furnishing of a product. The term information technology includes computers, ancillary equipment, software, firmware, and similar procedures, services (including support services), and related resources. [40 U.S.C., Sec. 1401]
Information Type	A specific category of information (e.g., privacy, medical, proprietary, financial, investigative, contractor sensitive, security management) defined by an organization or in some instances, by a specific law, Executive Order, directive, policy, or regulation. [FIPS 199]
Integrity	Guarding against improper information modification or destruction, and includes ensuring information non-repudiation and authenticity. [44 U.S.C., Sec. 3542]
Intelligence	(i) the product resulting from the collection, processing, integration, analysis, evaluation, and interpretation of available information concerning foreign countries or areas; or (ii) information and knowledge about an adversary obtained through observation, investigation, analysis, or understanding. The term 'intelligence' includes foreign intelligence and counterintelligence.

Intelligence Activities	The term 'intelligence activities' includes all activities that agencies within the Intelligence Community are authorized to conduct pursuant to Executive Order 12333, United States Intelligence Activities.
Intelligence Community	The term 'intelligence community' refers to the following agencies or organizations: (i) The Central Intelligence Agency (CIA); (ii) The National Security Agency (NSA); (iii) The Defense Intelligence Agency (DIA); (iv) The offices within the Department of Defense for the collection of specialized national foreign intelligence through reconnaissance programs; (v) The Bureau of Intelligence and Research of the Department of State; (vi) The intelligence elements of the Army, Navy, Air Force, and Marine Corps, the Federal Bureau of Investigation (FBI), the Department of the Treasury, and the Department of Energy; and (vii) The staff elements of the Director of Central Intelligence.
Lines of Business	"Lines of business" or "areas of operation" describe the purpose of government in functional terms or describe the support functions that the government must conduct in order to effectively deliver services to citizens. *Lines of business* relating to the <u>purpose</u> of government and the mechanisms the government uses to achieve its purposes tend to be mission-based. *Lines of business* relating to support functions and resource management functions that are necessary to conduct government operations tend to be common to most agencies. The recommended information types provided in NIST SP 800-60 are established from the "business areas" and "lines of business" from OMB's Business Reference Model (BRM) section of *Federal Enterprise Architecture (FEA) Consolidated Reference Model Document Version 2.3*
Low-Impact System	An information system in which all three security objectives (i.e., confidentiality, integrity, and availability) are assigned a FIPS 199 potential impact value of low. [FIPS 200]
Mission Critical	Any telecommunications or information system that is defined as a *national security system* (FISMA) or processes any information the loss, misuse, disclosure, or unauthorized access to or modification of, would have a debilitating impact on the mission of an agency.

Moderate-Impact System	An information system in which at least one security objective (i.e., confidentiality, integrity, or availability) is assigned a FIPS 199 potential impact value of moderate and no security objective is assigned a FIPS 199 potential impact value of high. [FIPS 200]
National Security Information	Information that has been determined pursuant to Executive Order 12958 as amended by Executive Order 13292, or any predecessor order, or by the Atomic Energy Act of 1954, as amended, to require protection against unauthorized disclosure and is marked to indicate its classified status.
National Security System	Any information system (including any telecommunications system) used or operated by an agency or by a contractor on behalf of an agency, or any other organization on behalf of an agency – (i) the function, operation, or use of which: involves intelligence activities; involves cryptologic activities related to national security; involves command and control of military forces; involves equipment that is an integral part of a weapon or weapon system; or is critical to the direct fulfillment of military or intelligence missions (excluding a system that is to be used for routine administrative and business applications, for example payroll, finance, logistics, and personnel management applications); or (ii) is protected at all times by procedures established by an Executive order or an Act of Congress to be kept classified in the interest of national defense or foreign policy. [44 U.S.C., Sec. 3542]
Non-repudiation	Assurance that the sender of information is provided with proof of delivery and the recipient is provided with proof of the sender's identity, so neither can later deny having processed the information. [CNSS Inst. 4009 Adapted]
Potential Impact	The loss of confidentiality, integrity, or availability could be expected to have: (i) a limited adverse effect (FIPS 199 low); (ii) a serious adverse effect (FIPS 199 moderate); or (iii) a severe or catastrophic adverse effect (FIPS 199 high) on organizational operations, organizational assets, or individuals. [FIPS 199]

Privacy Impact Assessment (PIA)	An analysis of how information is handled: (i) to ensure handling conforms to applicable legal, regulatory, and policy requirements regarding privacy; (ii) to determine the risks and effects of collecting, maintaining, and disseminating information in identifiable form in an electronic information system; and (iii) to examine and evaluate protections and alternative processes for handling information to mitigate potential privacy risks. [OMB Memorandum 03-22]
Public Information	Any information, regardless of form or format that an agency discloses, disseminates, or makes available to the public.
Risk	The level of impact on organizational operations (including mission, functions, image, or reputation), organizational assets, individuals, other organizations, or the Nation resulting from the operation of an information system given the potential impact of a threat and the likelihood of that threat occurring. [FIPS 200, Adapted]
Security Category	The characterization of information or an information system based on an assessment of the potential impact that a loss of confidentiality, integrity, or availability of such information or information system would have on organizational operations, organizational assets, individuals, other organizations, or the Nation. [FIPS 199, Adapted]
Security Controls	The management, operational, and technical controls (i.e., safeguards or countermeasures) prescribed for an information system to protect the confidentiality, integrity, and availability of the system and its information. [FIPS 199]
Security Objectives	Confidentiality, integrity, and availability.[FIPS 199]
Senior Agency Information Security Officer	Official responsible for carrying out the Chief Information Officer responsibilities under FISMA and serving as the Chief Information Officer's primary liaison to the agency's authorizing officials, information system owners, and information system security officers. [44 U.S.C., Sec. 3544]
Sensitivity	Used in this guideline to mean a measure of the importance assigned to information by its owner, for the purpose of denoting its need for protection.

Sub-functions	*Sub-functions* are the basic operations employed to provide the system services within each area of operations or line of business. The recommended information types provided in NIST SP 800-60 are established from the "business areas" and "lines of business" from OMB's Business Reference Model (BRM) section of *Federal Enterprise Architecture (FEA) Consolidated Reference Model Document Version 2.3*
System	See Information System.
Telecommunications	The transmission, between or among points specified by the user, of information of the user's choosing, without change in the form or content of the information as sent and received.
Threat	Any circumstance or event with the potential to adversely impact agency operations (including mission, functions, image, or reputation), agency assets, individuals, other organizations, or the Nation through an information system via unauthorized access, destruction, disclosure, modification of information, and/or denial of service. [CNSS Inst. 4009, Adapted]
Vulnerability	Weakness in an information system, system security procedures, internal controls, or implementation that could be exploited or triggered by a threat source. [CNSS Inst. 4009, Adapted]
Weapons System	A combination of one or more weapons with all related equipment, materials, services, personnel, and means of delivery and deployment (if applicable) required for self-sufficiency.

APPENDIX B: REFERENCES

S. 3418 [5 U.S.C. § 552A through Public Law 93-579], 93rd U.S. Cong., 2d Sess., *The Privacy Act of 1974*, December 31, 1974 (effective September 27, 1975).

S. 244 [Public Law 104-13], 104th U.S. Cong., 1t Sess., *Paperwork Reduction Act of 1995*, May 22, 1995.

S. 1124, Division E [Public Law 104-106], 104th U.S. Cong., 2d Sess., *Information Technology Management Reform Act of 1996*, February 10, 1996.

H.R. 3162, Titles VII and Title IX [Public Law 107-56], 107th U.S. Cong., 1t Sess., *The USA PATRIOT Act of 2001*, October 26, 2001.

Public Law 107-296, *Critical Information Infrastructure Act of 2002*, §§211-215, November 25, 2002.

H.R. 2458 [Public Law 107-347], 107th U.S. Cong., 2d Sess., *E-Government Act of 2002*, December 17, 2002.

H.R. 2458, Title III [Public Law 107-347], 107th U.S. Cong., 2d Sess., *Federal Information Security Management Act of 2002*, December 17, 2002.

Executive Office of the President, *Presidential Decision Directive 63, Protecting America's Critical Infrastructures*, May 22, 1998.

United States Office of Management and Budget, Circular No. A-130, Appendix III, Transmittal Memorandum #4, *Management of Federal Information Resources*, November 2000.

United States Office of Management and Budget, *OMB Guidance for Implementing the Privacy Provisions of the E-Government Act of 2002*, September 29, 2003.

United States Office of Management and Budget (OMB), Federal Enterprise Architecture (FEA) Program Management Office (PMO), *FEA Consolidated Reference Model 2.3*, October 2007.

United States Department of Commerce, National Institute of Standards and Technology, Federal Information Processing Standards Publication 199, *Standards for Security Categorization of Federal Information and Information Systems*, December 2003.

United States Department of Commerce, National Institute of Standards and Technology, Federal Information Processing Standards Publication 200, *Minimum Security Requirements for Federal Information and Information Systems*, March 2006.

United States Department of Commerce, National Institute of Standards and Technology, Special Publication 800-18, *Guide for Developing Security Plans for Federal Information Systems*, Revision 1, February 2006.

United States Department of Commerce, National Institute of Standards and Technology, Special Publication 800-30, *Risk Management Guide for Information Technology Systems*, July 2002.

United States Department of Commerce, National Institute of Standards and Technology, Special Publication 800-34, *Contingency Planning Guide for Information Technology Systems*, June 2002.

United States Department of Commerce, National Institute of Standards and Technology, Special Publication 800-37, *Guide for the Security Certification and Accreditation of Federal Information Systems*, May 2004.

United States Department of Commerce, National Institute of Standards and Technology, Special Publication 800-39, *Draft Managing Risk from Information Systems: An Organizational Perspective*, April 2008.

United States Department of Commerce, National Institute of Standards and Technology, Special Publication 800-53, *Recommended Security Controls for Federal Information Systems*, Revision 2, December 2007.

United States Department of Commerce, National Institute of Standards and Technology, Special Publication 800-53A, *Guide for Assessing the Security Controls in Federal Information Systems*, July 2008.

United States Department of Commerce, National Institute of Standards and Technology, Special Publication 800-59, *Guideline for Identifying an Information System as a National Security System*, August 2003.

United States Department of Commerce, National Institute of Standards and Technology, Special Publication 800-64, *Security Considerations in the Information System Development Life Cycle*, June 2004.

www.ingramcontent.com/pod-product-compliance
Lightning Source LLC
Chambersburg PA
CBHW060506060326
40689CB00020B/4657